SHIRE NATURAL H

THE
ADDER

PETER STAFFORD

CONTENTS

COVER: *A male Adder in breeding colours.*

Series editors: Jim Flegg and Chris Humphries.

Set in 9 point Times roman and printed in Great Britain by C. I. Thomas & Sons (Haverfordwest) Ltd, Press Buildings, Merlins Bridge, Haverfordwest, Dyfed.

Introduction

The Adder, also known as the Viper, is Britain's only poisonous snake. Of the three kinds of snake found in Britain, the Adder, because of its bite, is perhaps the best known, but despite many stories to the contrary, this sun-loving denizen of open heaths and commons is rather timid by nature and hardly deserves its villainous reputation.

The Adder, known scientifically as *Vipera berus,* belongs to the most sophisticated and evolutionarily advanced family of snakes alive today, the Viperidae, which contains some of the most poisonous snakes in the world. It could also be described as the most successful of all snakes, for although it is cold-blooded and must still rely on the heat of the sun for warmth, it appears to be more tolerant of low temperatures than do other species and as a consequence has been able to spread over much of northern Europe and Asia, ranging from the Atlantic coast of Britain and western Europe across Russia to the Far East, and from Italy northwards to Scandinavia and Finland within the Arctic Circle. The name 'Adder' originally comes from the old Anglo-Saxon word *naedre,* meaning a creeping thing.

There are approximately 2700 different species of snake, of which the dangerously poisonous varieties comprise some 10 to 15 per cent and are grouped into three main families according to the nature of their venom-injecting apparatus; the Colubridae, Elapidae and Viperidae. The Colubridae is composed mainly of harmless types but also contains some poisonous ones with a pair of venom-conducting fangs set in the rear of the upper jaw *(opistoglyphous).* Only a very few of these are dangerous to man. The Elapidae contains such formidable and deadly creatures as cobras, mambas, coral snakes and kraits, and the Viperidae includes, among others, the vipers and rattlesnakes. Snakes of the last two families all have a set of venom-conducting teeth in the front of the upper jaw, but while those of elapid species are largely immovable *(proteroglyphous),* the fangs of vipers and their relatives are hinged at the base and able to fold back along the roof of the mouth when the jaws are closed *(solenoglyphous).* This makes it possible for the viper's leading teeth to be substantially longer than would otherwise be practical, enabling the snake to bite deeper into its prey and the venom to disperse more effectively. Some of the large ground-dwelling vipers for example, such as the Gaboon Viper *(Bitis gabonica)* from Africa, possess fangs almost 2 inches (50 mm) in length, although those of the Adder by comparison are only about ¼ inch long (4 to 7 mm). Each fang can be operated independently of the other, and for protective purposes both are sheathed in a pocket of skin, together with a cluster of replacements held in reserve for when fangs break off or are shed, as happens naturally from time to time. The fangs themselves are tubular in structure, with a small hole just above the tip through which venom is squirted as the snake bites. Snake venom is produced and stored for use in a pair of modified salivary glands, located just beneath the eyes, and is supplied to the conducting teeth when required through a special duct.

There are nine genera of true vipers (subfamily Viperinae). Those of the genus *Vipera,* to which the Adder belongs, are all viviparous, producing live offspring, and are particularly unusual in that many are sexually dimorphic, males being coloured somewhat differently to females. Eight of the ten species which the genus embraces occur in Europe, and the Adder is perhaps most closely related to two of these in particular, the Aspic Viper *(Vipera aspis)* and the Meadow Viper *(Vipera ursinii),* both of which are very similar in appearance and may even interbreed.

SENSES AND ANATOMY

The best developed sense in snakes is that of smell, although scent particles in the air are not detected with the nose as they would be with mammals and birds, but by a special olfactory structure in the roof of the mouth, known as *Jacobson's organ,* which works in collaboration with the tongue. Smells are identified from samples of air collected on each occasion the tongue is protruded and withdrawn, and if the snake is highly aroused, for example when it is frightened or in pursuit of prey, the tongue can be seen to flicker in and out constantly as the snake tries to gather as much information about its surroundings as possible. To a lesser extent the tongue is also used as a tactile organ.

Vision in snakes is generally quite well developed, but by human standards most species are rather short-sighted. The eyes, it would appear, are thoroughly perceptive only of movement, and a snake hunting its prey by sight will often fail to recognise a suitable meal unless it begins to move, even if it is only a few inches away. Snakes do not have eyelids. Instead the eyes are covered with a single transparent scale, the *brille*, through which the snake is able to see quite clearly and which gives some degree of protection.

It is well known that snakes cannot hear in the same way as higher animals, the popular example being the snake charmer whose snake responds not to the music of his flute but to the movements he makes while playing it. Snakes have neither an external ear nor an eardrum, although they are still able to detect some sounds by way of vibrations transmitted to the inner ear via the bones of the lower jaw.

Vipers of the subfamily Crotalinae, including the pit-vipers and rattlesnakes, have another means of sensing prey. On each side of the face they have a heat-receptive pit, and it has been shown that some species, using these sensors, can strike accurately at moving warm-blooded prey even with their eyes blind-folded.

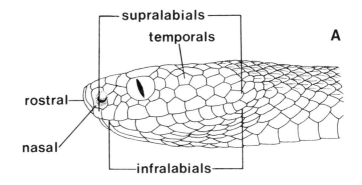

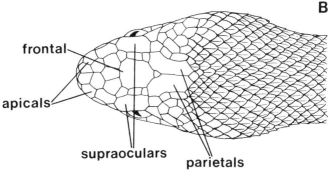

1. *Head scales of the Adder: lateral view, A; dorsal view, B. The top of the head is covered with numerous small granular scales, while those of the Grass Snake and Smooth Snake by comparison are more symmetrical and much larger, comprising nine main plates.*

3

The skin of snakes, and of all other reptiles, is composed largely of a horny and rather inflexible substance called *keratin,* the uppermost layer of which needs to be shed every so often to allow for growth. The frequency with which this layer is shed depends primarily on the rate of growth, and young healthy snakes, which feed more regularly and grow more quickly, will shed their skins more often. In the initial stages of moulting, or *sloughing* as the process is known, the skin loses its shiny lustre and the eyes turn milky-white in colour through the secretion of a lubricant beneath the layer of dead skin. During this time the snake is not able to see properly and may hide away and not feed again until its sight has been restored. This condition lasts only for a few days and soon afterwards the snake begins to rub its snout against the ground or over some other rough object in an effort to break through the old skin, which eventually splits and peels back over the rest of the body as it crawls along.

The entire surface of a snake's body is covered with scales, the arrangement and numbers of which are often used to help distinguish between different species. On the dorsal surface these scales are usually small and roughly triangular in shape, sometimes with a horizontal keel through the centre, while in most snakes those on the underside are larger and run crosswise in a single row from the neck to the base of the tail.

During the process of evolution, the size and position of the snake's internal organs have needed to change in line with the elongation and compression of its body, although in most other respects the organs themselves are not very different from those of man. The digestive tract in particular has probably undergone the most significant modification in order to cope with the ingestion of relatively large meals, and in some species the stomach alone can account for one-third of the total length. Also, to facilitate swallowing, the bones of the skull have become flexible and loosely hinged, and the lower jaw bones are designed to separate, making it possible for the snake to consume animals that would otherwise be far too large. The lungs have also been subject to change. In adopting such a narrow and elongate form, the left lung of many species, including the vipers, has become greatly reduced and no longer serves any useful purpose, although in some more primitive species both lungs remain functional and of almost equal size. The heart is somewhat different from that in higher animals, having only three chambers rather than four, and the male reproductive organ is an elaborate paired structure, covered with frills and hooks to prevent withdrawal during copulation.

As might be expected of an animal so long and with no limbs, a snake's skeleton is composed essentially of a vertebral column and framework of ribs. Some primitive species also possess vestigial remains of what at one time formed the pelvic girdle and hind limbs, and in certain groups, like the giant pythons and boas (family Boidae), the very ends of what is left of them can be seen at the base of the tail, protruding through the skin like small claws.

LOCOMOTION

Snakes can move in a number of different ways, as determined by their size, habits and habitat. The Adder and many other ground-dwelling species normally move rather slowly in an almost straight line, using the powerful muscles on the underside to push themselves along in a manner reminiscent of a caterpillar. Other species move by stretching out the forepart of their body and then pulling the rest up behind them, and some desert species have developed a way of shuffling sideways to move across loose sand. The most effective means of progression, as used by the more agile species of snakes, is the normal serpentine method, whereby the animal moves in an S-like fashion, using the curves of its body to gain leverage on any irregularities in the ground and thrust itself forward. By this means the body always follows the exact route taken by the head, giving the impression that movement is effortless and so graceful as to appear uncanny.

The speed with which snakes move is the subject of much conjecture and exaggeration. On level ground the Adder can

2. Typical colouration of an adult male Adder. Males are generally more brightly coloured than females, especially in the breeding season.

3. The female Adder tends to be more reddish or brownish in colour than the male and the markings are less distinct. Females also grow to a larger size.

maintain a speed comparable with the slow walking pace of a man, and over short distances it can move a little more quickly, although in rough country large and agile snakes can be at more of an advantage and move with greater ease than could a human. One of the fastest of all snakes is the deadly poisonous Black Mamba *(Dendroaspis polylepis),* which in its natural habitat of dry bush and rocky country has been known to exceed speeds of over 10 mph (16 km/h).

Identification, behaviour and ecology

While other and more dangerous species of viper occur on the mainland of Europe, the Adder is the only snake of its kind in Britain and can be easily distinguished from the two other native snakes, the Grass Snake *(Natrix natrix),* the only egg-laying British species, and the Smooth Snake *(Coronella austriaca).* The Grass Snake grows to a much larger size than the Adder, measuring up to 4 feet (120 cm), and is more a snake of damp meadows, freshwater pools and marshland, although it is occasionally found in much drier habitats. Ordinarily it is greenish brown or olive-grey above with an irregular series of black spots on the back and an evenly spaced row of vertical black bars on the sides. The main feature by which this snake can be identified is the presence of a bright yellow patch on each side of the neck, bordered to the posterior by a black crescent-shaped marking. With few exceptions this particular marking is more or less always present but in older or very young specimens it may be less obvious and not so easy to see. The underparts of the Grass Snake are usually whitish, heavily chequered with black.

The Adder is more likely to be confused with the Smooth Snake, whose general appearance is in some respects superficially similar. This animal, measuring about 2 feet (60 cm) when fully grown, is found only in certain parts of Dorset, Hampshire, Wiltshire, Surrey and Sussex but favours the same sorts of habitats as the Adder and the two are often to be found together. It is generally light brown, greyish or red-brown in colour, relieved by a pattern of small dark spots or short cross-bars on the back and a secondary series of spots on the sides, which may fuse towards the neck, producing a bold streak extending right through the eye. The ventral surface is grey or reddish brown and may be heavily mottled with pale spots or perfectly uniform.

The Adder differs most obviously from these two snakes in having a bold zigzag stripe extending the entire length of the back. Compared to a Grass Snake or Smooth Snake of similar size, the Adder is also more heavily built and on closer examination it can be seen that the character and arrangement of scales on the head are quite different. Another difference is that the Adder has elliptical eye pupils rather than round ones, as is the case with the other two species, although it is not a nocturnal reptile as this would normally imply.

The only other animal that might possibly be mistaken for the Adder is the Slow-worm *(Anguis fragilis),* a kind of legless lizard commonly found in the same areas as Adders. In form and movement the Slow-worm is deceptively snake-like, having an elongated body and no visible limbs, but it differs significantly from snakes in possessing movable eyelids and a fixed lower jaw. The body is also not as supple as in snakes, and the scales are much smoother, giving the animal a highly polished appearance. Slow-worms grow to a maximum length of about 16 inches (40 cm), and males and females differ in colour when fully grown. Females are generally a pale brown, reddish-brown or bronze colour above with a distinct longitudinal stripe along the back and another broad stripe on the sides. Males on the other hand are almost always much darker and more uniform in colour. The undersides of both sexes are blackish, sometimes finely spotted with grey.

All three native British snakes are found in mainland Europe as well as in Britain, where the Adder and Grass Snake in particular occur in several different colour forms. Only the Adder, however, shows any marked variation in colour and pattern within the British Isles. As mentioned earlier, it is one of the very few species of snake in which the sexes are coloured differently. On the whole, adult males tend to be more brightly coloured than females, ranging from dirty yellow through various shades of cream and grey to silvery white, with much bolder dorsal markings. In the breeding season these colours can be especially vivid. Females are normally a dull reddish brown or yellow-brown when fully grown, with less clearly defined markings.

In addition to the zigzag-like stripe on the back, both sexes also have a series of rounded or oval blotches on the sides and an X- or V-shaped marking on the back of the neck. A dark streak extends backwards from the eye to the angle of the jaw, and the underparts can either be grey, bluish, brown or black, with or without paler spots. In some individuals the underside of the tail is bright red or orange, but this is not particularly common. The iris of the eye is fiery red or copper-coloured.

Infant and juvenile Adders are coloured somewhat differently to adults, tending to be orange-brown or more reddish, especially the females. This appearance is gradually lost as they become sexually mature, but at one time it was mistakenly thought that these young red Adders were a separate species.

It is not only the ground colouration of Adders that can vary. Dorsal markings as well, especially on the back of the neck, seem never to be the same in any two individuals and may even be completely lacking. In some specimens the dark zigzag marking on the back dominates the upper surface, while in others the marking may be perfectly straight, broken into blotches, or take the form of a thin wavy line.

Perhaps the most striking colour variation of the Adder is the all-black or melanic form, in which the upper surface of the body is black or very dark brown. This unusual variety is not as uncommon as might be thought, and while few are completely black they are said to be quite numerous in certain parts of Britain. Albino Adders have also been recorded on occasion in Britain, but these are extremely rare and, being highly conspicuous, seldom survive long in the wild.

The Adder is not a large snake, rarely exceeding 2 feet (60 cm) in length. Males are generally smaller, averaging approximately 20 inches (50 cm), but some females are known to have attained lengths of up to 28 inches (70 cm), and in exceptional cases over 30 inches (76 cm). Growth is most rapid during the first five years of the Adder's life, after which it will have reached about 18 inches (46 cm), and then proceed to grow at a much slower rate. The male reaches sexual maturity at about two or three years old, females being able to reproduce in their third year. By most accounts the Adder can live for at least fifteen years and according to some authorities may even be able to exceed 25 years.

As with all other reptiles, the Adder is not able to control its body temperature in the same way as warm-blooded animals can and is largely dependent on the heat of the sun for warmth. In order to keep alert and be able to perform the activities of hunting, feeding and mating, it must first of all raise its body temperature to a level at which it can function properly, and this it achieves by lying out in the sun. On particularly cool days Adders will spend much of their time just basking lazily in a sheltered patch of sunlight, but during midsummer, when average temperatures are higher, they are able to remain active virtually all day long without needing to bask.

Because the Adder cannot maintain an adequate body temperature through its own metabolism it must hibernate during the winter months to avoid the freezing cold in which it would otherwise soon perish. As the days of autumn grow colder and shorter, the Adder becomes increasingly lethargic, finally going into hibernation about the end of September or the beginning of October, depending on the prevailing weather. Shelter is normally sought among the roots of heather and small shrubs, or in disused

4. *The Grass Snake (Natrix natrix) is quite different from the Adder in appearance and can be immediately distinguished by the black and yellow collar behind the head.*

5. *It is sometimes possible to mistake the Smooth Snake (Coronella austriaca) for the Adder, although only in southern Britain, to which this species is restricted.*

6. *Not a snake but a legless lizard, the Slow-worm (Anguis fragilis), although snake-like in appearance, can be readily identified by its striped dorsal pattern and highly polished scales.*

rodent burrows, or in any suitable nook or cranny protected from flooding and where the frost cannot penetrate. In particularly favourable places large numbers of Adders may congregate in a communal den, sometimes along with the animals on which they would otherwise normally feed.

MATING AND REPRODUCTION

The first priority for the Adder when it comes out of hibernation in the spring is mating and reproduction, although it must first spend a few days basking in the sun as much as possible to re-acclimatise its body. Adult male Adders emerge first, normally appearing towards the end of March, with females and juveniles following between two and five weeks later, although Adders have been known to emerge as early as February, with snow still on the ground. At about this time the female gives off a scent from a pair of glands at the base of the tail for the purpose of attracting a mate. A trail of this scent is left behind as she moves around and is easily detected by any interested male in the vicinity. Seeking her out by smell, the male at once becomes engrossed in a highly spirited courtship ceremony, following the female's movements exactly and continuously flicking his tongue in and out over her body, a performance which may last for several hours before copulation finally takes place. Should a rival male appear on the scene, the courting male will immediately give chase, racing alongside the intruder in a heated confrontation which ultimately terminates in a spectacular event often called the 'dance of the Adders', whereby the two snakes rise up against each other, their bodies interlaced, and attempt to force one another to the ground. The display is frequently accompanied by exaggerated swaying movements of the body and finally ends when one of the contestants gives in and bolts for cover. Neither snake ever tries to bite the other.

Female Adders tend to breed every other year. The gestation period lasts for between three and four months, the young being born at the end of August or beginning of September. New-born Adders are encased in a transparent membrane at birth, which ruptures when the young snake thrusts and pushes against the side with its head. The number of offspring produced varies according to the size of the female, the average litter containing from five to fourteen, each measuring around 6 to 8 inches (15-20 cm). The ratio of males to females in each litter is fairly equal. Young Adders may stay with the mother for some days after being born, although they are capable of looking after themselves and also of giving a poisonous bite. They do not usually begin to feed until some time later when the embryonic yolk supply has been completely used up. Until the late nineteenth century it was believed that in times of danger baby Adders would be swallowed by the mother for protection, but this has been proved not to be the case. The story might have arisen from the fact that baby Adders will sometimes wriggle under the parent for safety, and to a startled onlooker it may have seemed as though they were disappearing down her throat. Even after detailed scientific investigation many influential naturalists of the day remained unconvinced, although this behaviour has never been photographed, nor has a live Adder ever been caught with its brood in its gullet.

FEEDING

In common with most other snakes, Adders can survive without food for considerable periods of time and yet not suffer from any harmful effects or lose any significant weight. Their reserves of body fat, built up during the summer, enable them to sleep through the winter without needing to feed, and also provide sustenance in the spring when they are more preoccupied with courtship and mating than with finding a meal. The Adder's diet consists in the main of small mammals and reptiles, principally mice, voles, shrews and lizards. They will also take fledgling birds and possibly any other animal of suitable size if given the

7. An Adder devouring a bank vole. Prey is swallowed whole and always head first. The lower jaw is able to dislocate from the other bones of the skull, and the skin stretches like elastic, enabling such large prey items to pass beyond the throat and into the digestive tract with relative ease.

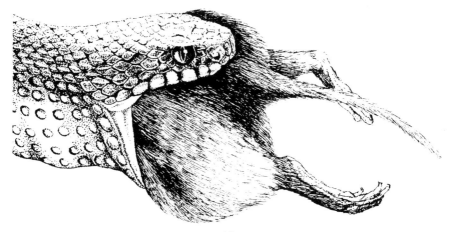

opportunity. An Adder has been photographed trying to consume the chick of a Merlin. Juvenile Adders feed largely on the young of the animals they would prey upon as adults, these being predominantly small lizards and new-born rodents.

If sufficiently hungry, the Adder will not hestitate to capture any small animal that wanders close enough or happens to cross its path, but its usual method of hunting is to go in search of prey, moving stealthily through the undergrowth until it catches sight of a suitable meal or picks up its scent. Sampling the air with its tongue as it goes and creeping steadily forward, it proceeds to stalk the animal until it reveals itself by moving. Then, edging closer to within a few inches of it, the Adder slowly draws the forepart of its body into an S-shaped loop and at precisely the right moment strikes out with lightning speed, biting and releasing its hold all in the same fraction of a second. The wounded animal is quick to react and dives for cover in a bid to escape, but within two or three minutes the venom will have taken effect and rendered the unfortunate creature helpless. Knowing that it will not have gone very far, the Adder takes time to compose itself and then slowly heads off to where its intended meals lies dead or dying, following its trail by means of smell. Not every time will the Adder's first attack be successful, however, and quite often it will have to stalk its prey several times before it can get in a position to deliver its lethal bite. Small and fast-moving animals like mice and voles, which would normally be too quick and alert to be caught above ground, are usually pursued into their burrows to be killed.

Prey is always swallowed in one piece, and as quickly as possible, although it is nonetheless a fairly slow process and animals the size of a large vole may take up to half an hour or so to consume. After it has finished the Adder retires to digest its meal and will not usually want to feed again for about three or four days.

In common with other terrestrial animals, the Adder needs to drink water from time to time, especially during hot weather, to replenish moisture lost by evaporation through the skin. Some fluid is undoubtedly obtained from its prey, but the Adder will also drink regularly and copiously from streams and puddles, dipping its snout below the surface and drawing in water through the notch from which its tongue normally protrudes. It may also obtain moisture from droplets of dew or rainwater if there is no permanent water supply to hand.

DISTRIBUTION AND HABITAT

In Britain the Adder occurs generally throughout England, Scotland and Wales, but it is not found in Ireland and is also absent from the Orkneys, Shetlands, Outer Hebrides and the Isle of Man. There are certain areas where, because of the nature of the land, they are noticeably more abundant, but over Britain as a whole they appear to be no more plentiful in southern England than in the north of Scotland. In southern parts, however, they are generally restricted to smaller areas and so may seem more prolific. In the south of England, the heathlands of Exmoor, Dartmoor and the New Forest are especially noted for Adders, as are the Downs of Sussex and Kent and parts of Dorset and Somerset. The Adder has been described as locally abundant in the Midlands and in Wales, especially on the Gower peninsula, in the mountainous districts of Powys and Dyfed, and in many coastal areas. It tends to be less common in the east of England, where the landscape is not so much to its liking, but to the north in parts of the Lake District and Yorkshire Dales it is plentiful. In Scotland, where Adders are the only snakes to be found, they are said to be widespread and particularly common in the glens and mountains of Inverness and Easter Ross.

The Adder is usually regarded as a snake of dry sandy heaths, but it can also be found in pine and deciduous forest, reed beds, old quarries, on moorland, sand dunes and rocky hillsides, along disused railway cuttings and in a host of other places. It has even been reported that Adders have been seen basking on the roofs of thatched cottages, however unlikely this may be. It appears that Adders most frequently occupy two different kinds of habitat during the time of year they are active, and these snakes in

8 (left). *Black Adders can occasionally be seen in Britain and in some parts are said to be locally common. Few are ever completely black, however, and there is usually some trace of a pattern on the back or a reddish patch under the throat.*

9 (below). *The Adder moves by contracting the muscles on the underside backwards from the neck in a rippling action, termed horizontal undulatory locomotion. In movement the head is always carried slightly above the ground. Adders normally travel at a speed comparable with the slow walking pace of a man. Over short distances they can move a little faster but tire very quickly.*

10 (right). *Male rivalry in the spring. Two male Adders rise to confront each other over possession of a female. (Photograph by J. van der Rijst.)*

11 (below). *Infant Adders are often more reddish than mature snakes, changing to their adult colouration in about their fourth or fifth year of life. At one time they were thought to represent a different species, the 'Dwarf Red Adder'.*

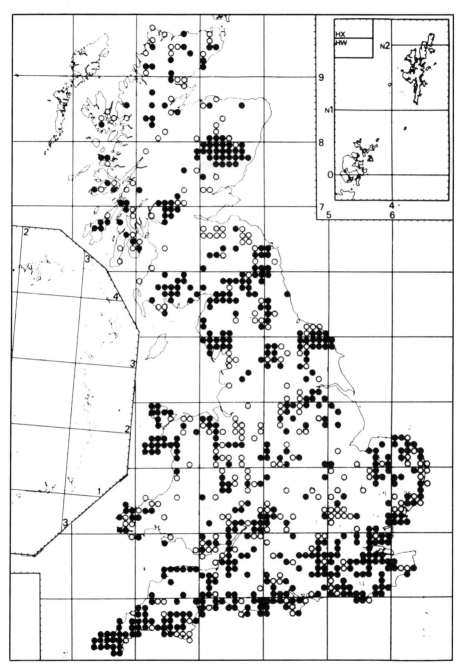

12. *Distribution of the Adder in Britain. Unshaded circles represent records made before 1960.*

14

particular seem to have a well developed sense of direction. In spring, up to about the middle of May, they stay in the vicinity of the hibernation area, usually a dry south-facing bank covered with low herbage, where mating takes place and the males perform their running battles in competition for females. They may then travel some distance away and disperse into lower-lying, often wet country, such as damp river meadows, waterlogged heaths or even the edges of blanket bogs, and here they remain for the best part of four months, occupied mostly with hunting and feeding. Towards the end of August they make their way back to the same hiberation site, where the females give birth, a journey which may be up to a mile (1.6 km) in distance and take several days.

DISEASE AND ENEMIES

Adders are not troubled to any great extent by parasites and disease in the wild, and neither do they have many natural enemies. They are most frequently eaten by predatory birds, such as buzzards, owls, crows and ravens, but other animals including hedgehogs and polecats will also prey upon them. The most significant casualty rate is undoubtedly brought about by the activities of man. In particular, the clearance of large tracts of heathland for cultivation and urban development has led to a substantial decline in the numbers of Adders, and they have even disappeared entirely from areas where they were once abundant. Whereas many animals eventually grow to ignore being disturbed by humans, it seems that the Adder will still flourish only in those areas where its privacy and solitude are most likely to remain uninterrupted, and this often explains why an otherwise perfect habitat will turn out to be devoid of them. During the summer Adders may also be killed on the roads by motor vehicles, or by the seasonal burning of heathland, and it seems that man himself will still kill them indiscriminately even in this conservation-orientated age. Severe winters may also take a large toll of Adders in hibernation, especially young ones born the previous autumn, and it is estimated that through natural means approximately 88 per cent of all infants die within the first three years of life.

The Adder is not an aggressive animal by nature and in captivity is even said to become quite tame. If accidentally trodden on or molested in any way, however, it will defend itself violently, hissing loudly and striking repeatedly.

Watching Adders

To go out into the field with the intention of finding a poisonous snake is not something to be undertaken lightly, and Adders should always be treated with the greatest of respect. It is, however, quite possible to observe Adders in their natural surroundings without having to approach them too closely, and providing no attempt is ever made to catch these snakes or provoke them there should never be any danger of being bitten.

Although locally common in many areas, the Adder is not an animal that one might expect to go out and find straight away. As they are hidden by their camouflage and very particular in their choice of habitat, looking for these elusive reptiles and being able to spot them before they see you requires concentration and at first a great deal of patience.

Whatever the type of habitat, Adders are most likely to be seen while basking, and for this they invariably choose a sheltered position well exposed to the sun and conveniently close to some kind of cover into which they can dive for safety at a moment's notice. To the casual observer an area of heath, commonland or an overgrown embankment may look quite uninteresting and much the same all over, but in certain places the vegetation will be thicker, affording better protection, or the incline against the sun more advantageous for basking, and it is in these sorts of 'niches' that Adders tend to be found. Most frequently selected as basking sites are the tops of grassy

13. 'Dance of the Adders'. In what amounts only to a show of strength, the two males, their bodies interlaced and heads held high, pursue each other in a heated chase which finally ends when one of the contestants gives in and bolts for cover. (Photograph by J. van der Rijst.)

tussocks, small openings amid bracken, gorse or bramble bushes, on the sunny edge of paths between clumps of heather, and at the bases of sapling trees, where refuge can be quickly found under the roots. Fallen logs, heaps of dry bracken and molehills are also much favoured, and the snakes may even climb into the branches of small bushes some distance from the ground. In particularly suitable basking places, especially in early spring and autumn when the weather is cooler, Adders may congregate in considerable numbers, and up to nineteen have been seen sunning themselves on the same spot.

Probably the most effective way of looking for Adders on open heath or commonland is to walk slowly amongst the vegetation, pausing every now and then to scan the surrounding area for signs that snakes may be present, such as old discarded skins or the animals on which they would feed. At the same time a sharp lookout should be kept for movements in the herbage, suitable basking places or the snakes themselves, and for this a pair of binoculars is often useful. It is particularly important not to tread too heavily, as although snakes are largely 'deaf' to airborne sounds they are nonetheless extremely sensitive to ground vibrations and can be easily disturbed. The habitat in which they live should always be left the way it is found and not unnecessarily trampled on. It is often more productive to follow the paths already made by other animals, such as sheep or deer, where the flattened ground affords ideal basking opportunities, rather than struggle through dense herbage. As rather sensitive creatures, the snakes and their way of life should be disrupted as little as possible, especially during the early part of the year when courtship and mating are under way.

Adders can sometimes be observed simply by watching and waiting. If not frightened too seriously, an Adder disturbed from the place where it lay basking will often return to the same spot, or very near it, within just a few minutes, giving time to take up position at a suitable distance and to be prepared for when it reappears. In this way it is often possible to observe the snakes and their habits at close quarters, providing an excellent opportunity to take photographs. This can be especially rewarding in the spring when they are busily engaged in courtship and mating activities.

To avoid making any accidental noise or sudden movements, a small stool such as a shooting stick often comes in useful.

With such a bold pattern it might be thought that Adders would be conspicious and easy to see, but the markings serve rather to break up the outline of the snake, helping it to blend with its surroundings and conceal itself from predators and prey. As it lies motionless on a tussock of grass, clump of heather, or amongst dry bracken, its camouflage is extremely effective and it is often only when the snake begins to move that it becomes visible. Even then it may not be possible to catch more than a brief glimpse before it disappears from view. Where Adders do occur, however, they are often to be found in some numbers, and with patience it should eventually be possible to spot more of them before they take fright and sneak away.

Adders can sometimes be found by listening for movements in the undergrowth. The continuous rustling noise

14. *After a brief courtship the triumphant male is able to mate with the female. Copulation may last for several hours and the male may mate with a number of females. (Photograph by J. van der Rijst.)*

15. *Most frequently selected as hibernation sites are south-facing banks covered with low herbage, where the snakes may overwinter together in large numbers. From this embankment in Dorset over twenty Adders emerged one year after hibernation.*

they make when crawling through dead leaves or grass is surprisingly loud and is easy to distinguish from the more intermittent scuffling sounds made by lizards, mice and other small animals. Similarly, on a calm day Adders can also be located by watching for the movements they make in tall grass, especially in the spring when they are busy chasing each other in courtship or rivalry. By watching for the places where the grass parts and sways, the route of an Adder can be traced as it moves along, even though the animal itself may not be visible.

There are certain times of the day and year when Adders are more likely to be seen than at others. In early spring when they first emerge from hibernation they may lie out in the sun for much of the day, making the most of whatever heat is available. At this time of year the vegetation is also sparse and much shorter, making it easier to spot them, and because the weather is cooler they are often more reluctant to move from their basking places and can sometimes be approached quite closely. Having not long emerged from hibernation, the Adders are collected more or less all in one area. When the weather turns cooler in the autumn, they may again spend long periods sunning themselves out in the open before the approach of winter finally drives them underground.

Adders will not be much in evidence on windy days or if the weather is cold and overcast, but they can sometimes be found out and about on thundery days when the atmosphere is warm and humid. Even if the weather conditions should be somewhat unfavourable, female Adders, heavy with offspring in late summer, may come out to take advantage of whatever little heat there is to help incubate their developing broods.

When the Adder first emerges in the morning it will usually lie outstretched with its body flattened at right angles to

16. *On heaths and open commonland Adders hibernate in the highest and driest parts, seeking shelter under the ground among the roots of trees or bushes, or in old rabbit warrens. This type of habitat is characterised by such plants as heather (Erica spp.), ling (Calluna vulgaris) and Wavy-hair Grass (Deschampsia flexuosa), with a scrub layer of brambles (Rubus fruticosus), gorse (Ulex spp.), bracken (Pteridium aquilinum) and sapling birch trees (Betula pendula).*

17. *When courtship and mating are over, Adders may travel some distance and disperse into lower-lying, often wet country, characterised by a different mixture of plants, including sedges (Carex spp.), coarse tuft-forming grasses, and, in the wettest parts, reeds (Phragmites and Juncus spp.) and sphagnum mosses. It is in areas of this sort during the summer where much of their hunting and feeding is undertaken.*

18. *Camouflaged amongst the heather and gorse, a male Adder catches the last of the autumn sunshine before retiring into hibernation. When the weather is cool Adders may lie out in the open for much of the day, lazily basking in the sun, although never too far from where they can quickly find shelter.*

the sun, absorbing as much warmth as possible. After a while it normally takes up its more usual basking position, in a loose circular coil. Adders will not usually come out until the air temperature rises above 50 F (10 C) and seldom become very active until warmed to at least 68 F (20 C). If the day remains cloudy, with only short or intermittent periods of sunshine, they may not be tempted out at all. They are most likely to be seen on days when the air is calm and the weather warm and sunny. On such days in high summer they may emerge to bask as early as 7 o'clock in the morning and within an hour or so be fully active, although it is not a good idea to start looking for them too soon after sunrise as the vibration caused while moving around might easily deter them from coming out altogether. During very hot spells there is little point in looking for them after midday, by which time they will have normally disappeared in seach of shade.

Adders in folklore

That such a small and relatively insignificant creature as an Adder could be capable of inflicting a painful bite must have seemed shocking to the inhabitants of ancient Britain, and it is perhaps not surprising that this reptile, above all others, features prominently in myth and superstition. Its bite in particular has lent itself to much hocus-pocus, and by to-day's standards some of the early remedies with which it was treated seem not only bizarre but crude in the extreme. Most of these were based on an oil' or powder made from the Adder or some part of its anatomy, usually the fat, which was either melted down to make an ointment or cut from the fresly killed snake and applied directly to the wound.

The raw fat was also used to treat ordinary cuts and burns. An oil made from the Adder's liver, or the whole snake itself, was commonly used to treat the bite, and in parts of Surrey it would be carried by shepherds out to the pasture to treat any sheep that were bitten. Probably the most unsavoury cure for adder-bite was that used in Scotland, where a live pigeon would be torn to pieces and its warm flesh rubbed into the wound to extract the venom.

Through the ages a wide range of other ways has been devised to treat adder-bite, including the following selection of concoctions described in a book entitled *The British Sportsman, or Nobleman, Gentleman, and Farmer's Dictionary,* written by William Augustus Osbaldistone in 1792: 'I, garlic, onions, bacon and baysalt all stamped together; II, cover the wound with Venice treacle or mithridate; III, apply stamped rue, mustard seed, pickled herrings, black soap, deer's suet and bear's grease.'

Other derivatives of the Adder also had their medicinal uses, such as the cast skin, which, wrapped around the head, was said to be an effective cure for headache.

There are many tales about the Adder which have their origins in local superstition. The village folk in some parts of Devon, for example, once believed that if an Adder were to bite a cow its exact shape would be reproduced in the cream when the animal was next milked, and around Newcastle Emlyn in Wales it was believed that if a spider could be persuaded to crawl over the back of an Adder the snake would immediately destroy itself and be rendered completely harmless. Perhaps more extraordinary, it was said of Adders in Lincolnshire that to obtain a meal they would position themselves under larks soaring in the sky and then spit poison at them, killing the birds so that they would circle down and drop straight into the snake's open mouth.

Early man in Britain had some very strange ideas about the Adder and its way of life. In prehistoric times it was believed that young Adders killed their mother when coming into the world, and any human found guilty of such a crime would be tied up in a bag with one of these baby snakes and drowned as a punishment. The association of Adders with 'snake stones' is also very old. Legend has it that around Midsummer's Eve these and other snakes would gather in a particular place and by joining their heads together and hissing would produce a kind of bubble. This bubble would then be blown through the gullet of one of the snakes and expelled in the shape of a ball, which after it had hardened was said to look like a glass ring and bring good luck to anyone who found it. A variation of the same story was once told around Glamorgan, whereby the snakes would kill one of their kin and on its tail weave a small ball, which would bring prosperity and good fortune to whoever found it.

Some of the ways suggested to keep Adders from entering places frequented by humans have been equally bizarre. To remove them from gardens, for example, it was said they could be discouraged by planting wormwood, an aromatic herb, or by placing a well beaten mixture of 'onions and river crabfish' at the place where they were last seen. It was also recommended that the area be smoked by burning hartshorn, lily roots, old shoes or ash-tree boughs still in leaf, and this may contain an element of truth for Adders, in common with all snakes, dislike smoke or pungent fumes of any sort.

Effects and treatment of adder-bite

As a snake which is rather timid by nature and only seldom seen, it might be thought that the Adder and its poisonous bite would not be difficult to avoid, but accidents happen every year for which treatment and sometimes even hospitalisation are necessary. It is in the south of Britain where most cases of adder-bite occur, almost always among holidaymakers who take to the countryside when the weather is warm and sunny; young children, being naturally inquisitive are especially vulnerable. In a small number of cases the bites are received accidentally, usually through stepping on an Adder or putting a hand on one while picking flowers or climbing a bank, but by far the majority are caused by deliberately trying to catch or even kill one of these snakes and pick it up.

The most frequent victim of adder-bite in Britain, however, is not man but the domestic dog, which may inadvertently come across the snakes while running about over rough heath or commonland. Most at risk are sporting breeds, such as terriers, hounds and spaniels, which have the habit of scrambling through dense vegetation and poking their noses into the recesses and holes where Adders tend to hide. It is not always possible to tell straight away if and where a dog has been bitten, but within half an hour or so the affected part, usually the nose or a paw, begins to swell and the dog quickly becomes tired with any physical effort. Animals thought to be suffering from the effects of adder-bite should be taken to a veterinary surgery for examination as soon as possible, so that treatment and advice on aftercare can be given. Dogs bitten by Adders usually take at least a week to recover but very rarely succumb to the effects of the venom, even if left untreated. The area around the bite may swell to an alarming size, although it usually returns to normal after two or three days and can sometimes be further relieved by bathing with a solution of witch-hazel. Cows and other farm animals also get bitten occasionally, but hardly ever with fatal consequences.

Snake venoms are basically made up of various proteins and enzymes and generally speaking can be divided into two main groups; those which are *haemotoxic* in action, destroying the red blood cells and causing haemorrhage of the vessels, and those which attack the nervous system bringing about death through paralysis of the heart and lungs, termed *neurotoxins*. The constituents and properties of venom differ considerably between each individual species, but most vipers and rattlesnakes possess what is

19. *Venom-injecting mechanism of the Adder: f, functional fang; m, maxilla; p, pterygoid; rf, reserve fangs; vd, venom duct; vg, venom gland. When the mouth is opened to bite, the pterygoid bones on each side of the head move forward, rotating the paired maxillae clockwise and erecting the fangs into a vertical position ready for use. The jaws are opened to an angle of almost 180 degrees and, as the snake bites, venom is squeezed by muscular action through the venom duct and injecting fang into the wound. Only the functional fang receives venom. The nearest reserve fang moves forward and is ready to receive venom the moment the old fang is shed.*

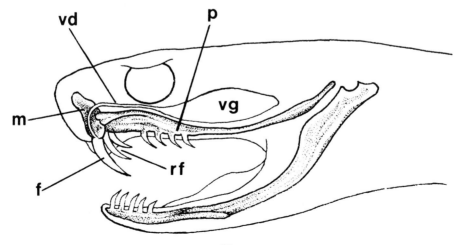

chiefly a haemotoxic poison, while cobras, mambas and other elapid species are predominantly neurotoxic.

Amongst poisonous snakes the Adder is not a particularly dangerous species and, although something to be avoided, its bite is not as lethal as that of many other venomous snakes. In its normal state, as a liquid, the venom is a pale amber in colour and tends to become more potent the longer it remains unused. At one bite the snake can inject about 0.01 cc, which is sufficient to kill within minutes the small animals on which it feeds, but unlikely to cause anything more than local pain, swelling and nausea in a healthy adult.

The severity of adder-bite in man, however, varies considerably and is dependent on such criteria as the size of the snake, the amount of venom injected and the age and health of the victim. After the initial pain of the bite, some time may elapse before the first noticeable signs of its effect become apparent, although not usually more than an hour. Inflammation of the bitten part may follow, together with oedema, further swelling and a throbbing ache in the region of the bite, but if only a small amount of venom was injected these may be the only symptoms to develop. In more severe cases the swelling is accompanied by tenderness under the arms and in the groin, a rise in temperature, giddiness, vomiting, drowsiness and diarrhoea. The victim may also perspire heavily although at the same time complain of feeling cold. Discolouration of the skin in the vicinity of the bite almost always occurs, and in particularly severe cases large pieces of dead tissue may later slough off. Other symptoms include loss of appetite and an unusual thirst due to the dehydrating effect of the venom. In more extreme cases the victim may temporarily lose consciousness and then complain of being unable to breathe or swallow properly. There may also be abdominal pain and difficulty in co-ordinating movements of the limbs, and if bitten on a finger or toe haemorrhagic blisters may develop in the region of the bite. The effects of envenomation usually reach a peak within six to 48 hours, and depending on the severity it is usual to make a complete recovery within one to two weeks.

Rather than use antivenom to treat adder-bite, most medical practitioners in Britain nowadays prefer to use other methods, such as antibiotics and antihistamines, or a blood transfusion, and even these may only be used if it is felt there is a definite need. With improved processing techniques, the risk of allergic reaction to antivenom serum is now much reduced, but at one time it was believed to be more dangerous than the bite itself.

Adder-bites in man which result in death, however infrequent and exceptional they may be, have and sometimes still do occur. Over the last one hundred years or so only about a dozen such cases have been recorded in Britain, almost all of them children below the age of fifteen. The younger and smaller the victim, the more serious it would appear are the effects of envenomation, but elderly victims and those suffering from delicate health may also be at more of a risk.

FIRST AID

In the event of being bitten by an Adder, the victim should at once seek medical aid. The bitten part should be immobilised with either a splint or a bandage, and to impede the absorption of venom as little physical effort exerted as possible. Children should be carried if transport is not available. It is generally not advisable to make an incision across the wound and apply suction, or use a tourniquet, as the risk of infection and possibly gangrene is thereby increased. For the same reason strong caustic solutions should not be used. Above all the victim should be reassured. To alleviate shock there is no harm in giving hot drinks of tea or coffee, but on no account should alcohol be offered. The snake responsible should not be caught to confirm identification, as further bites may be received; the Adder is in any case the only native British snake capable of giving a poisonous bite and the symptoms of envenomation will soon become apparent.

Places to visit

British reptiles, including the Adder, are sometimes to be seen on display at the following centres:
Dartmoor Wildlife Park, Sparkwell, Plymouth, Devon. Telephone: Cornwood (075 537) 209.
New Forest Reptiliary, near Lyndhurst, Hampshire. Ordnance Survey 1:50,000 map 195, grid reference 271071.
Poole Aquarium and Serpentarium, Blue Boar Mill, The Quay, Poole, Dorset. Telephone: Poole (0202) 686712.
Welsh Mountain Zoo and Botanic Garden, Colwyn Bay, Clwyd, Wales. Telephone: Colwyn Bay (0492) 31660.

Further reading

Appleby, L. G. *British Snakes.* John Baker, 1971.
Arnold, E. N., and Burton, J. A. *A Field Guide to the Reptiles and Amphibians of Europe.* Collins, 1978.
Arnold, H. R. (editor). *Provisional Atlas of the Amphibians and Reptiles of the British Isles.* Biological Records Centre, Monks Wood, Natural Environment Research Council, 1973.
Frazer, D. *Reptiles and Amphibians in Britain.* Collins, 1983.
Hinxman, L. W. 'Notes on the Common Adder in the Highlands'. *Annals of Scottish Natural History* (1902), 151-3.
Kochva, E., and Gans, C. 'The Structure of the Venom Glands and Secretion of Venom in Viperid Snakes'. In *'Animal Toxins',* Pergamon Press, 1967.
Morton, C. B. 'Adder Bites in Cornwall'. *British Medical Journal,* volume 1 (1960), 373-6.
Phelps, T. *Poisonous Snakes.* Blandford Press, 1981.
Prest, I. 'An Ecological Study of the Viper *Vipera berus* in Southern Britain'. *Journal of Zoology,* volume 164 (1971), 373-418.
Prior, H. T. J. 'The Dance of the Adders. A Remarkable Example of Reptilian Rivalry'. *Countryside,* volume 9 (1933), 492-3.
Service, R. 'The Adder in Solway'. *Annals of Scottish Natural History,* (1902), 153-62.
Smith, M. *The British Amphibians and Reptiles.* Collins, fifth edition 1973.
Steward, J. W. *The Snakes of Europe.* David and Charles, 1971.
Vesey-Fitzgerald, B. 'Some Notes on Vipers'. *Proceedings of the Hampshire Field Club,* volume 16 (1946), 197-206.

ACKNOWLEDGEMENTS

Illustrations are acknowledged as follows: H. R. Arnold (updated map 1985) 2; C. Andrén and G. Nilson 8; J. van der Rijst, 10, 13, 14. All other illustrations are by the author. For various courtesies grateful thanks are also due to J. R. Billingsley and A. F. Stimson.